preteen Bible study series

How to Make Great Choices

Loveland, Colorado

Group's R.E.A.L. Guarantee to you:

This Group resource incorporates our R.E.A.L. approach to ministry—one that encourages long-term retention and life transformation. It's ministry that's:

Relational
Because learner-to-learner interaction enhances learning and builds Christian friendships.

Experiential
Because what learners experience through discussion and action sticks with them up to 9 times longer than what they simply hear or read.

Applicable
Because the aim of Christian education is to equip learners to be both hearers and doers of God's Word.

Learner-based
Because learners understand and retain more when the learning process takes into consideration how they learn best.

preteen Bible study series

How to Make Great Choices

Copyright © 2003 Group Publishing, Inc.

Visit our Web site: **www.grouppublishing.com**

Credits
Authors: Steve Bridges, Steven B. Huddleston, and Steve and Annie Wamberg
Editor: Jim Hawley
Creative Development Editor: Karl Leuthauser
Chief Creative Officer: Joani Schultz
Copy Editor: Lyndsay E. Gerwing
Art Director: Kari K. Monson
Cover Art Director/Designer: Jeff A. Storm
Cover Photographer: Daniel Treat
Print Production Artist: Tracy K. Hindman
Illustrator: Shawn Banner
Production Manager: DeAnne Lear

ISBN 0-7644-2481-5
10 9 8 7 6 5 4 3 2 1   12 11 10 09 08 07 06 05 04 03

Printed in the United States of America.

Contents

Introduction:
How to Make Great Choices

oug's mother was shocked when the doctor told her that Doug had an ulcer. "An *ulcer*? He's only twelve years old!" she told the doctor.

As Doug explained some of the pressures he was facing at school—trying to decide between playing in band or playing baseball and losing interest in math but really enjoying reading lately, to name only two—his mom began to realize the pressure he was under.

Preteens today face many tough choices in all areas of their lives. *How to Make Great Choices* will help preteens discover how God can help them make choices in the most important areas they face. In the first study, they'll explore how God guides them. They will discover that God has a purpose for each of their lives and how he guides them in that purpose.

Next, preteens will examine the things they make priorities in their lives. They will explore how God's priorities are the most important and how to integrate his priorities with their own.

> Preteens today face many tough choices in all areas of their lives.

In the third study, your students will explore a hot topic—media—and how to evaluate media choices—such as TV, movies, music, computer games, and the Web—in light of God's standards. They will discover how to avoid harmful media choices in their lives.

Sometimes, preteens face hard choices due to circumstances in which they find themselves. The last study will help them focus on God and keep a good attitude with God's help when they find themselves in difficult situations. Preteens will discover how God can use the tough times in life to strengthen faith.

About Faith 4 Life: Preteen Bible Study Series

The Faith 4 Life: Preteen Bible Study Series helps preteens take a Bible-based approach to faith and life issues. Each book in the series contains these important elements:

• **Life application of Bible truth**—Faith 4 Life studies help preteens understand what the Bible says and then apply that truth to their lives.

• **A relevant topic**—Each Faith 4 Life book focuses on one main topic, with four studies to give your students a thorough understanding of how the Bible relates to that topic.

• **One point**—Each study makes one point, centering on that one theme to make sure students really understand the important truth it conveys. This point is stated upfront and throughout the study.

• **Simplicity**—The studies are easy to use. Each contains a "Before the Study" box that outlines any advance preparation required. Each study also contains a "Study at a Glance" chart so you can quickly and easily see what supplies you'll need and what each study will involve.

• **Action and interaction**—Each study relies on experiential learning to help students learn what God's Word has to say. Preteens discuss and debrief their experiences in large groups, small groups, and individual reflection.

• **Reproducible handouts**—Faith 4 Life books include reproducible handouts for students. No need for student books!

• **Flexible options**—Faith 4 Life preteen studies have two opening and two closing activities. You can choose the options that work best for your students, time frame, or supply needs.

• **Follow-up ideas**—At the end of each book, you'll find a section called "Changed 4 Life." This provides ideas for following up with your students to make sure the Bible truths stick with them.

Use Faith 4 Life studies to show your preteens how the Bible is relevant to their lives. Help them see that God can invade every area of their lives and change them in ways they can only imagine. Encourage your students to go deeper into faith—faith that will sustain them for life! Faith 4 Life, forever!

Seeking God's Guidance

The Point: ➤ God guides our lives with his purpose.

P reteens are being pressured into making tough decisions as they face new challenges in school and with peers and increased responsibility and freedoms at home. They may struggle to know the right choices to make, adding stress and confusion to their young adolescent years.

Use this study to show preteens ways to seek and find guidance from God as he works his purpose for their lives.

Scripture Source

Genesis 12:1-7, 10; 13:1-4, 14-18; 17:1-8

God tells Abram to leave his land in Ur and go to the place he will show him. Abram builds altars to the Lord along various resting places during his long journey. God promises Abram that his descendants will be more than he can count as they inherit the land from the river of Egypt to the Euphrates River.

Isaiah 53:6

Isaiah tells the people that they are like sheep and have strayed from God's way.

1 Thessalonians 1:4-6

Paul reminds his fellow Christians how the Holy Spirit helped them to know Jesus and his message as they lived out their lives.

2 Timothy 3:16-17

Paul explains to Timothy that Scripture is inspired by God and will provide the guidance and correction all people need.

Hebrews 11:8

Abraham's faithfulness is recorded in the Hebrew author's honor roll of faithful people. Abraham obeyed God and left his land to set out for the Promised Land.

James 1:5-6

James tells his fellow Christians that they can ask God for wisdom and he offers it freely.

The Study at a Glance

Section	Minutes	What Students Will Do	Supplies
Warm-Up Option 1	up to 10	**Story Ending**—Finish an open-ended story about two boys in a dangerous situation.	
Warm-Up Option 2	up to 10	**Puzzling Directions**—Complete a puzzle with and without directions.	"Word Puzzle" handout (p. 14), scissors, envelopes, paper
Bible Connection	up to 20	**Abraham's Guidance**—Experience what Abraham's journey to Canaan was like and discuss God's guidance.	Bibles, paper, markers "Abraham's Journey" map (p. 15)
	up to 10	**How God Guides**—Examine various Scriptures about how God guides them.	Bibles, paper, pens, newsprint, marker
Life Application	up to 10	**Faithful Guidance**—Examine personal ways they need God's guidance and pray for a partner's need.	Bible, index cards, pens
Wrap-Up Option 1	up to 5	**God's Will for *Good***—Reflect on ways they haven't been seeking God's will in their lives.	Bible, slips of paper, pens
Wrap-Up Option 2	up to 5	**God's Faithful Protection**—Reflect on how God's faithfulness can encourage them to continue to trust him.	

Before the Study

Set out Bibles, paper, pens, newsprint, markers, and index cards. Also make enough photocopies of the "Abraham's Journey" map (p. 15) for each preteen to have one. Make four photocopies of the "Word Puzzle" handout (p. 14), and prepare them as explained on page 9.

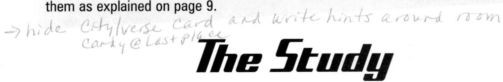
→ hide City/verse card and write hints around room
candy @ Last place

The Study

Warm-Up Option 1

1/22 ①

Story Ending *(up to 10 minutes)*

Read the following story to the group:

Kirk and Todd were in the mood for adventure. They were familiar with the old town legend that a treasure was hidden deep inside the old Hollow Fork Cave. Today, they decided, would be the day they found that old treasure. If they had bothered to ask their parents, they would have been warned not to go near the dangerous cave, but they didn't ask. On the way to Hollow Fork,

they met Mr. Reeves, an old man and family friend. When he asked the boys where they were off to, they just said they were going exploring. Had they mentioned to Mr. Reeves their intentions to go in the old cave, he could have explained to them how the myth of the treasure was started years ago. He could even have told them how his own brother was killed in that very cave when they were boys. But they never gave him a chance to warn them. As Kirk and Todd entered the mouth of the cave, they walked right past a big sign. If they had taken the time to read it, they would have learned that the cave was prone to rapid and dangerous flooding. But they didn't bother to read the sign. Kirk and Todd went into the cave, armed only with their flashlights.

After climbing and crawling between rocks for about an hour, they suddenly heard a strange noise...

Stop reading, have kids form pairs, and give pairs three to five minutes to decide the story ending and its consequences with their partners.

When time is up, have each pair share its story ending and the consequences. Discuss the motives for the warnings and the various ways the two boys could have avoided the consequences.

Say: When we neglect to follow instructions and warnings for our lives, we are apt to suffer consequences. Today we're going to explore how God has instructions for our lives as well. ➤God guides our lives with his purpose. Let's see how following his guidance will bless our lives.

◄ *The Point*

Warm-Up Option 2

Puzzling Directions *(up to 10 minutes)*

Before the study, make four photocopies of the "Word Puzzle" handout (p. 14), and cut out the puzzle pieces from three of the handouts. Place the cut pieces of each handout in a separate envelope.

Have kids form three groups, and give each group an envelope with a set of puzzle pieces. Also give each group a sheet of paper on which to place the puzzle pieces. Spread out groups so they can't see what the other groups are doing. **Say: When the pieces are arranged properly, they'll reveal something that God is to every believer. Let's see which group can put the puzzle together first. You'll have five minutes.**

Students will almost certainly not be able to solve the puzzle. After a few minutes, give a copy of the handout with the directions to one of the groups. Whisper to the group members that when they have solved the puzzle, they may verbally tell one other group the secret if another group asks them.

Ask: • **What was it like trying to complete this puzzle? Explain.**

• **If I gave your group the instructions, how did that make the puzzle easier?**

• **How did it feel to be told the answer by another group? Explain.**

• **Do you think you could've done the puzzle without my or another group's instructions? Why or why not?**

Show groups who haven't completed the puzzle how to solve it. **Say: The word in the puzzle is** *guide*, **which is what God is to us.** ➤**God guides our lives with his purpose. Let's see how following his guidance will keep us from making a giant "puzzle" out of our lives.**

The Point ➤

Bible Connection

Students find city, read verse, answer question about verse and receive next hint

Abraham's Guidance *(up to 20 minutes)*

1/22 (2)

Before the study, plan a route on which you'll take students to simulate Abraham's journey. If the weather is nice, plan your route outside, if possible. Make signs, and write the following Bible references on each sign:

Haran: Genesis 12:1-3

Shechem: Genesis 12:4-7

Egypt: Genesis 12:10

Bethel: Genesis 13:1-4

Hebron: Genesis 13:14-18

Canaan: Genesis 17:1-8

Place the signs in order, allowing a minute or so of travel time between the sign locations. Have the last stop on your route, Canaan, near to your room, if possible. Place the first sign, Haran, in your room or meeting area. Give a photocopy of the "Abraham's Journey" map (p. 15) to each person.

(3) 1/22 Discussion — **Say: Thousands of years ago, God had a special plan for a man named Abraham. Let's experience Abraham's journey as we look for how God guided him.**

Provide Bibles for volunteers who would like to read the Scripture passages along the route. Lead preteens over to the first place, and ask the volunteer to read the passage indicated on the Haran sign (Genesis 12:1-3). Point out Haran on the map. **Say: The journey of Abram (who was later renamed Abraham) began here when he was seventy-five years old.**

Ask: • **How would you feel if you were Abram and God told you to leave your country and go to an unknown place?**

Say: Abram followed God's guidance and left. Let's see where he went.

Lead preteens to the next stop on the route you laid out. When you arrive, point out the place on the map, and have a volunteer read the Scripture passage listed on the sign. Repeat the same procedure for the remaining places on the route. After you've done this at the last place (Canaan), return to your room. **Say: We covered over twenty years of Abram's life and the many hundreds of miles he traveled in a few minutes on our route. God even changed Abram's name to Abraham as he guided him in his journey.**

Have students form pairs or trios and discuss these questions:

Ask: • **What do you think it would've been like to have experienced Abraham's journey?**

• **How did God guide Abraham along his journey?**

• **How did Abraham respond to God when he arrived in the various places along his journey?**

• **How has Abraham's journey helped you see how God can guide your life?**

Say: God probably won't speak to you and me the way he spoke to Abraham. But just as God guided Abraham's life with his plan, ➤**God guides our lives with his purpose. Let's explore ways he does this today.**

◀ *The Point*

How God Guides *(up to 10 minutes)*

Have kids form three groups, and assign each group one of the following three Bible passages: 1 Thessalonians 1:4-6; 2 Timothy 3:16-17; or James 1:5-6. Give each group a Bible, a sheet of paper, and a pen. Have groups choose a reader who will read the Scripture to the group, a recorder who will write down the group's findings, a reporter who will share the group's findings with the class, and one or more encouragers to keep everyone focused. **Say: In your groups, read your assigned passage, and discuss how you see God's guidance in your passage. You'll report your findings in a few minutes.**

Give groups about four minutes to research their passages. Then have reporters share their groups' discoveries. Record each group's responses on newsprint with a marker.

Ask: • **How do these Bible passages help you see God's guidance?**

FYI

Whenever groups discuss a list of questions, write the questions on newsprint, and tape the newsprint to the wall so that groups can discuss the questions at their own pace.

FYI

If you have more than fifteen students, have kids form six groups, and assign the same Scripture to two groups. If you have fewer than nine students, combine some of the roles within each group—for example, the reader can also be the reporter.

• What are some other ways you think God guides us?

Say: These passages have helped us see how God guides us through his Word, his Holy Spirit, and the influence of other Christians. Now let's think about how we need God's guidance.

Life Application

Faithful Guidance *(up to 10 minutes)*

The Point ➤

2/5 #5

Ask a volunteer to read Hebrews 11:8 aloud. **Say:** ➤**God guides our lives with his purpose, just as he guided Abraham. When God told Abraham to leave his land, Abraham obeyed. God will guide us, but only as much as we let him. We must choose to be faithful to his guidance. When we are, God's purpose for our lives will unfold.**

Have students form pairs, and provide index cards and pens. Have each partner think of a way he or she needs God's guidance and write that down on his or her card. Then have partners exchange cards and pray for their partners' needs.

Ask: • **Was it easy or hard to think of a way you need God's guidance? Explain.**

• **What things can you do to discover God's purpose for your life?**

• **How can you be more faithful to God's guidance in your life?**

Say: Our faithfulness in seeking God's guidance for our lives is important. Let's close our study by committing our faithfulness to God.

Wrap-Up Option 1

2/5 #6

discus
Give examples
of how
(before)) ↑
(scattagories style)
A
1
2

God's Will for *Good* *(up to 5 minutes)*

Say: God's will or purpose for us is always what is good for us. God may not be guiding us because we aren't seeking what is *good*.

Ask a volunteer to read Isaiah 53:6 aloud. Give kids slips of paper and pens. Have them each write one area in their lives that has "gone their own way" *any* and hasn't been God's will. Also write one way yourself.

Have kids form a circle, and place a trash can in the middle. **Say: We're going to go clockwise around the circle, and each person will say, "God, help me follow your way" or something similar. Then toss your paper into the trash can as a commitment and prayer to God to follow his way. I'll start and also conclude the prayer when we've completed the circle.**

last - Crab style
Soccer
w/ Nerf ball

Repeat the prayer, and toss your paper into the trash. Have the person on your left continue the prayer. When everyone has prayed, close the prayer, asking for God's guidance.

Wrap-Up Option 2

God's Faithful Protection (up to 5 minutes)

Have kids form pairs. Have partners share with each other one time they were protected from harm because they followed God's guidance. Then have them share one time they received a blessing they would've missed had they not followed God's guidance.

Close with a prayer of thanks for God's protection and guidance.

Extra-Time Tips

Use these extra ideas to add some creative fun to your studies. They are low-prep or no-prep ideas that work in no time!

Command Performance—Tape a sheet of newsprint to the wall. Ask kids to brainstorm for one minute to see how many dos and don'ts from the Bible they can list. Then have students determine how each command can either protect us or provide for us. Write their answers on the newsprint next to the command.

Weave Through Chaos—Select a volunteer to blindfold and send through a maze of chairs. Divide the rest of the class evenly between those who give helpful instructions and those who will try to lead the volunteer off the path. Discuss the many "voices" kids hear when they are searching for God's purpose, and help kids determine how they can sift through the voices to find God's guidance.

Word Puzzle

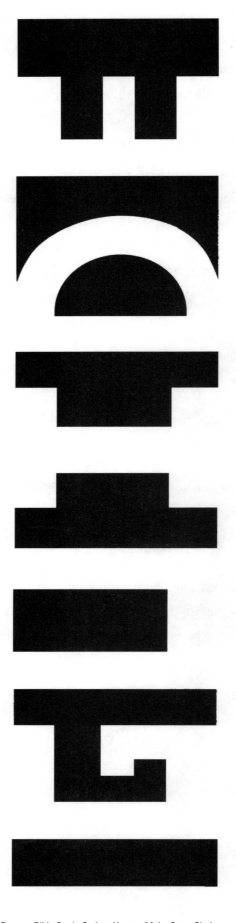

Abraham's Journey

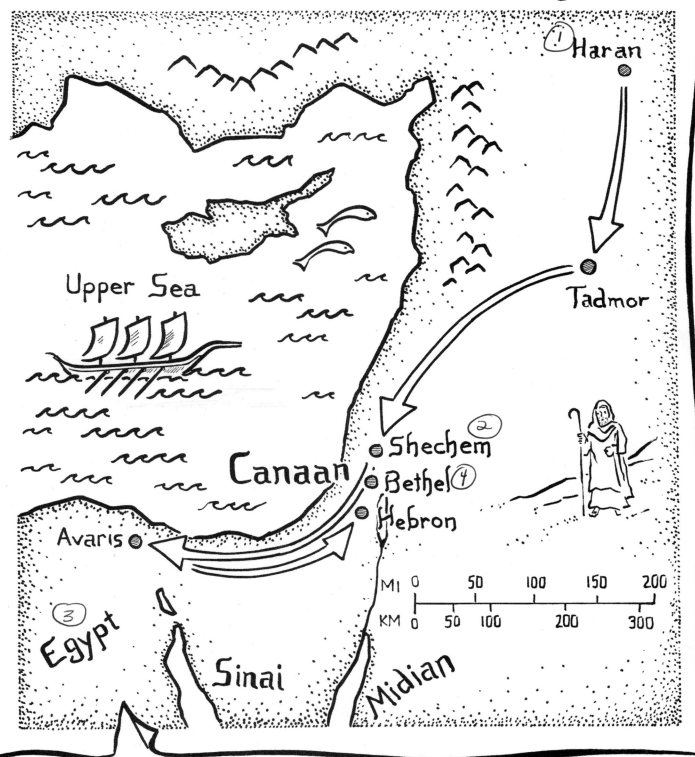

Haran ①

Tadmor

Upper Sea

Canaan

Shechem ②
Bethel ④
Hebron

Avaris

Egypt ③

Sinai

Midian

MI 0   50   100   150   200
KM 0 50 100   200   300

God-Pleasing Priorities

The Point: ➤ God helps us choose priorities that are pleasing to him and fulfilling for us.

As preteens mature, they may have a hard time determining what should be their priorities in life. While they are given more responsibility, they also have much of their lives that they feel they cannot control—school, chores, and family activities, for example.

Use this study to help preteens learn ways they can prioritize areas of their lives and to keep God as the most important priority.

Scripture Source

Matthew 22:35-40

Jesus identifies the most important commandment when asked by the Jewish religious leaders. The religious leaders almost seemed to revel in the abundance of laws they followed in order to be "righteous." From all these, Jesus singles out loving God as the first and greatest commandment.

Philippians 3:10-14

Paul explains the motivation behind his ministry. He knew the costs, and he understood the rewards. He had forsaken everything that made him who he was to become the person Christ had created him to be. And he did it all so he could know God and one day receive the "prize" that waited for him in heaven.

Philippians 4:13

Paul encourages Christians to trust in the strength the Lord provides, and with his strength, accomplish all things.

Colossians 2:6; 3:17

Paul writes to remind Christians to live in Jesus and that everything they say and do should be done in the Lord's name with thankfulness to God.

1 Peter 3:15

Peter encourages Christians to be prepared to share their hope in Christ with all who ask but to share in a kind and loving way.

The Study at a Glance

Section	Minutes	What Students Will Do	Supplies
Warm-Up Option 1	up to 5	**My Priorities**—List and discuss personal priorities.	Index cards, pens
Warm-Up Option 2	up to 10	**One Choice**—Decide what one material object is most important to them during a simulation.	
Bible Connection	up to 20	**Life Priority Stations**—Create priorities in several areas of their lives and evaluate them based on several Scriptures.	Bibles, "Personal Priorities" handout (p. 23), pens, paper, marker, tape
	up to 15	**Top Priority**—Examine Matthew 22:35-40 and Philippians 3:10-14 and determine what their number one priority should be.	Bibles, tape, newsprint, markers
Life Application	up to 10	**Life Priorities Revisited**—Re-examine their various life priorities in light of the top priority determined in the previous activity.	"Personal Priorities" handouts (used previously), pens
Wrap-Up Option 1	up to 5	**Priority Thanks**—Thank God for his help in making priorities.	"Personal Priorities" handouts (used previously)
Wrap-Up Option 2	up to 5	**Priority Motto**—Decide on a personal motto to help them keep their priorities in order.	Newsprint, marker, paper, pens

Before the Study

Set out Bibles, index cards, pens, newsprint, markers, and paper. Also make enough photocopies of the "Personal Priorities" handout (p. 23) for each preteen to have one.

The Study

Warm-Up Option 1

My Priorities (up to 5 minutes)

Say: **Today we're going to be talking about priorities.**

Distribute an index card and pen to each student. Say: **I want you to list on your cards three priorities you have for your life. A priority is like a goal. They can be from any area of your life—from school, home, or any interests you have. You might say you want to improve one letter grade in your weak school subjects, or you might spend more time practicing guitar. The priorities can be** in any order. You have two minutes. Begin now.

Allow two minutes for kids to write their priorities.

Ask: • **Was it easy or hard to create a list of your priorities? Explain.**

• **Do you think having priorities is important? Why or why not?**

• **What do you do to show that a priority is important to you?**

Say: **We make priorities for all aspects of our lives. And God cares about every aspect of our lives. Because of this, today we're going to look at how ➤God helps us choose priorities that are pleasing to him and fulfilling for us.**   ◀ *The Point*

Warm-Up Option 2

One Choice *(up to 10 minutes)*

Have kids form groups of up to four. **Say:** **Today we're going to be talking about priorities. To get us into the flow of this topic, we're going to conduct a simulation role-play.**

Lead kids into another room for the remainder of this activity. Once you've arrived, close the door. **Say:** **Each of you has contracted a rare and contagious disease. There is no cure, and doctors have given you only a few weeks to live. Because the disease is so contagious, you must remain in this room until you die. But you are allowed one thing to have with you. Talk with your group members, and decide what is the most important thing you will have. Each person may choose his or her own item.**

FYI

If you don't have another room available to you, simply lead your students out of your room and then re-enter to begin the simulation.

Allow a few minutes for each student to choose his or her one item. Have volunteers share their responses. **Say:** **In this simulation, you were placed in a serious situation. The choice you made showed that you placed a priority on having that one item with you. Although priorities in your normal lives probably won't be as drastic as our simulation, they are becoming increasingly more important as you mature. Today we're going to look at how ➤God helps us choose priorities that are pleasing to him and fulfilling for us.**   ◀ *The Point*

Lead your preteens back to your original room.

Bible Connection

Life Priority Stations *(up to 20 minutes)*

Before this study, set up five areas in your room or meeting area. Place a Bible at each station. Label five signs, and tape up one at each station. The five signs are

School Priorities, Family Priorities, Friendship Priorities, Fun Priorities, and Spiritual Priorities.

Have kids form five groups, and give each student a "Personal Priorities" handout (p. 23) and a pen. **Say: There are five stations set up around the room. Each of your groups will have two minutes to work on your priorities for that station. For example, if you go to the School Priorities station, you can discuss with your group what would be good priorities for succeeding in school. Each person can come up with his or her own priority or use one discussed in the group. Sometimes you'll need to use your own, while other times you can use the group's choices, depending on which priority you're working on. After two minutes, you'll rotate clockwise to the next station. After ten minutes, we'll discuss your responses as a large group. Use the Bible verses listed on your handout as inspiration as you set your priorities. There are also Bibles at each station if you want to look up another verse that is helpful to you while setting your priority.**

Ask four volunteers to each read one of the Bible verses on the handout. Answer any questions students may have about the activity, then have groups move to the stations. Give one-minute and thirty-second warnings, then have groups rotate to the next station after two minutes. Repeat this procedure for the remaining three stations. After the final station, have groups gather.

Ask: • What did you discover as you chose priorities?

• Were some priorities harder than others? Explain.

• How were the Bible verses helpful in setting your priorities?

• Were some priorities more important to you than others? Explain.

Say: Setting priorities in life is something that will become increasingly more important as you grow older. ➤God helps us choose priorities that are pleasing to him and fulfilling for us. As this activity showed, some priorities are more important than others. Let's look at the most important priority for our lives.

FYI

Whenever groups discuss a list of questions, write the questions on newsprint, and tape the newsprint to the wall so groups can discuss the questions at their own pace.

The Point ➤

Top Priority (up to 15 minutes)

Tape a sheet of newsprint to the wall, and title it "The Top Priority." Have kids form pairs, and assign each pair one of these two passages: Matthew 22:35-40 or Philippians 3:10-14. Have pairs look up and determine the "top priority" Christians should have based on their passages. As soon as pairs have an answer, have them come up to the newsprint, one pair at a time, and write it.

Ask: • Do you think these priorities could be called "top priorities"? Why or why not?

Say: Let's work together and narrow this down to one unified top priority.

Have preteens work together to combine all their answers into one unified top priority for all Christians. Have a volunteer write that priority at the top of the newsprint (or on another sheet of newsprint). **Say:** Let's see how to apply this top priority to our lives' priorities.

Life Application

Life Priorities Revisited (up to 10 minutes)

Provide pens, and have preteens form pairs or trios. Have kids retrieve their "Personal Priorities" handouts used earlier. **Say:** Now that we've determined a top priority, go back over the five areas on your handout, and evaluate them based on how well your life priorities fit the top priority. Then change or replace priorities that conflict with the top priority. Talk about your priorities with your partner(s) as you rework your lists.

Allow preteens a few minutes to work. When everyone has reworked their priorities, have groups discuss the following questions:

Ask: • How will including the top priority change the way you'll live out your new priorities?

• What's one thing you'll do this week to put your new priorities into practice?

Say: As we've explored today, ➤God helps us choose priorities that are pleasing to him and fulfilling for us. Let's thank God for helping us this way.   ◀ *The Point*

Wrap-Up Option 1

Priority Thanks (up to 5 minutes)

Gather kids in a circle. Have students bring their "Personal Priorities" handouts (used earlier) with them. Have students each choose one priority from their handouts that they want to offer to God in prayer. Go around the circle, and have each person say his or her priority as part of the prayer. Close after everyone has shared, thanking God for helping us choose ➤priorities that are pleasing to him and fulfilling for us.   ◀ *The Point*

Priority Motto *(up to 5 minutes)*

Have kids form groups of up to four, and have group members work together to create a motto to help them with their priorities. For example, kids could write, "Go for the prize; don't compromise." Provide paper and pens, and write group mottoes on newsprint as they share them with the class. Challenge kids each to pick one motto (or another if they have one in mind) and commit it to memory to use daily to help keep their priorities in order.

Close with prayer, thanking God for giving kids the courage to live their priorities.

Extra-Time Tips

Use these extra ideas to add some creative fun to your studies. They are low-prep or no-prep ideas that work in no time!

Priority Person—Ask kids each to tell the group the name of a friend or relative who makes it a priority to love and follow Jesus and why.

A World With No Priorities—Have kids brainstorm what they think a world without any priorities would be like. Help them discover the total chaos that would result in such a world.

Personal Priorities

School Priorities:

_____
_____
_____

Family Priorities:

_____
_____
_____

Friendship Priorities:

_____
_____
_____

Fun Priorities:

_____
_____
_____

Spiritual Priorities:

_____
_____
_____

"So then, just as you received Christ Jesus as Lord, continue to live in him" (Colossians 2:6).

"And whatever you do, whether in word or deed, do it all in the name of the Lord Jesus, giving thanks to God the Father through him" (Colossians 3:17).

"I can do everything through him who gives me strength" (Philippians 4:13).

"But in your hearts set apart Christ as Lord. Always be prepared to give an answer to everyone who asks you to give the reason for the hope you have. But do this with gentleness and respect" (1 Peter 3:15).

Verses to Live By

Media Messages and Me

The Point: ➤ God wants us to avoid harmful media choices.

Preteens are surrounded with many media choices today, including TV, movies, music, the Web, and computer games. Preteens are often exposed to media choices that are potentially harmful. Yet, as they mature, they are also able to question and wrestle with these choices.

Use this study to help preteens evaluate and choose positive media choices.

Scripture Source

Deuteronomy 11:18-20

God commands the Israelites to obey his words alone. To keep them from straying from the path he had chosen for them, God gave the Israelites clear guidelines for how he wanted them to live and how he wanted them to worship him. They were told to talk about God's Word as they woke up, went to sleep, and went about their day. The result would be God's wonderful blessing on their lives and the lives of their children.

2 Samuel 15:1-14; 18:9-15, 28-33

On a daily basis, Absalom, David's son, deceived the people of Israel using charm, flattery, and eloquent words. In time, he stole their hearts from King David. Absalom conspired against his father, trying to gain the throne. Eventually this led to Absalom's death, crushing his rebellion.

Philippians 4:8-9

Paul encourages Christians to focus on things that glorify God. He urges them to think about eternal things—things of beauty and value.

The Study at a Glance

Section	Minutes	What Students Will Do	Supplies
Warm-Up Option 1	up to 10	**New This Fall**—Create a poster for a new TV show.	Magazines, scissors, newsprint, colored markers, tape
Warm-Up Option 2	up to 10	**Instant Star**—Guess their secret media star identities.	Index cards, marker, tape
Bible Connection	up to 15	**Stealing the People's Hearts**—Play a game of persuasion and explore Absalom's rebellion in 2 Samuel 15.	Bibles, 2 crowns, candy snacks
	up to 15	**Measuring the Media**—Evaluate spiritual value of popular media in light of Philippians 4:8-9.	Bibles, "Media Messages" handout (p. 32), pens, newsprint, markers, tape
Life Application	up to 10	**The Word in Our Hearts**—Create media choice expressions based on Deuteronomy 11:18-20.	Bibles, newsprint, markers, paper, pens
Wrap-Up Option 1	up to 10	**Up With Media!**—Brainstorm positive things about media.	Newsprint, marker
Wrap-Up Option 2	up to 5	**Top Ten List**—Create a top ten list of media's good qualities.	Newsprint, marker

Before the Study

Set out Bibles, magazines, scissors, tape, index cards, two crowns, candy snacks, newsprint, markers, paper, and pens. Also make enough photocopies of the "Media Messages" handout (p. 32) for each preteen to have one.

The Study

FYI

It would be a good idea to check the appropriateness of the pictures in the magazines you use in this activity.

Warm-Up Option 1

New This Fall *(up to 10 minutes)*

Have kids form four groups. Give each group a stack of magazines, a pair of scissors, a sheet of newsprint, tape, and colored markers.

Say: Using your supplies, make a poster for a new TV show called *The Telly Family*. This show is about a family whose entire life is controlled by whatever they see on television. For example, if they see a diaper commercial, they'll immediately go buy some diapers, even if they don't have babies. Along with your poster advertising the show, create an idea for what a sample plot might include. You can choose any celebrities you want to star in your show, but be ready to explain why you chose whom you did.

Allow the groups five minutes to create their posters. Then have groups share their posters with the rest of the class.

Ask: • **Why did you choose the celebrities you did?**

• **How would you feel if you were starring in this show? Explain.**

• **How is this TV show like or unlike real life?**

Say: **Life may not be like this TV show, but the truth is that television, movies, and other media can have a powerful influence, both good and bad, on our lives. Today we're going to explore this and see how ➤God wants us to avoid harmful media choices.**

Warm-Up Option 2

Instant Star *(up to 10 minutes)*

Provide index cards, and have each student write the name of a media star, without letting anyone see what name is on his or her card. They can choose names of music, TV, or movie stars. Collect the cards, and have kids line up with their backs facing you. Mix up the cards, and tape one card to each person's back.

Say: **Let's play the Instant Star Game! Choose one person to talk to. Talk to each person as if he or she really is the star written on his or her card, without using the actual name. The object is for the person wearing the card to figure out who he or she is. For example, if your card says "Elvis," you need to figure that out by the way people are talking to you. If someone guesses correctly, both people should sit down.**

After everyone is sitting down, or after five minutes, stop the game.

Ask: • **How did you feel when you were being talked to like a media star? Explain.**

• **Which media stars do you wish you could be like? Why?**

Say: **We can learn a lot from this game about how we view famous performers. There may be times we want to be like them, but we don't know what they're really like. Today we'll explore media personalities and choices as we see how ➤God wants us to avoid harmful media choices.**

◀ *The Point*

Bible Connection

Stealing the People's Hearts *(up to 15 minutes)*

Choose two outgoing volunteers for this activity: one to play the role of King David and the other to play Absalom. Tell kids not to say their role-play names. Students will explore the story in detail after this skit, so they don't need to know the names of the characters. Put identical crowns on the volunteers' heads, and give Absalom the candy snacks. Put the volunteers on opposite sides of the room and the rest of the class in the middle.

Say: We're going to be exploring a story about a king and his son. Let's act out the first part of the story. You have to figure out which person you want to follow by choosing to side with one of them. Once you've made a decision, you can't change your mind. You are free to help your person gain additional followers.

Pull the volunteers aside, and give them the following instructions: During the game, David can only say, "God chose me to be the king" or similar phrases; Absalom can compliment the class, flatter them, make promises, and give out candy, while being as persuasive as possible.

After three to five minutes, stop the game and count who has the most followers.

Ask: • Was it easy or hard to choose which person to follow? Explain.

• Which person do you think would be trustworthier? Why?

Say: We've just acted out the first part of a true story from the Bible, in which King David's son, Absalom, conspired against him. Let's see what actually happened.

Have preteens form four groups, and have Group 1 read 2 Samuel 15:1-6, Group 2 read 2 Samuel 15:7-14, Group 3 read 2 Samuel 18:9-15, and Group 4 read 2 Samuel 18:28-33. Have groups read and summarize their passage. Then have a volunteer share his or her group's passage with the class, beginning with Group 1 and going in order for the remaining groups.

Ask: • After hearing the end of the story, how has your opinion of Absalom changed?

• What do you think Absalom's motive was?

• How are actions of media stars you know about similar to Absalom's?

• Are the actions or lifestyles of media stars important to you in your media entertainment choices? Why or why not?

FYI

Whenever groups discuss a list of questions, write the questions on newsprint, and tape the newsprint to the wall so that groups can discuss the questions at their own pace.

• **How do you think the people following Absalom were hurt when his rebellion failed?**

Say: We see lifestyles of media stars that may look great on the surface, but we don't always see the real-life consequences of those lifestyles. Just as Absalom charmed the hearts of the people away from King David, we can be charmed by the messages of the lifestyles or messages of media stars.
➤**God wants us to avoid harmful media choices. Let's examine some of the current media choices available to us.**

◄*The Point*

Measuring the Media *(up to 15 minutes)*

Ask a volunteer to read Philippians 4:8-9 aloud. **Say: The Apostle Paul gives us a good standard to measure our media choices with in these verses. Let's do that now.**

Give each student a "Media Messages" handout (p. 32) and a pen. Have kids form pairs, and give pairs Bibles. Have pairs look up Philippians 4:8-9 in their Bibles. **Say: In your pairs, decide on a media source for each of the four areas listed on your handout. For example, if you're evaluating a computer game, write the name of that game and then rate the game according to the eight qualities from the Philippians passage. Do this for all four media areas. Begin now.**

Give pairs about five to eight minutes to complete their handouts. While kids are working, tape up four sheets of newsprint, and label each sheet one of the four media choices on the handout: TV, Movies, Music, and Web or Computer Games. When students have finished their handouts, ask for volunteers to share results by giving their media source and the number of plus and minus signs for it. List at least two sources for each media category on the newsprint.

Ask: • **What surprised you about evaluating your media choices?**

• **Do you think it's important to evaluate our media choices? Why or why not?**

• **What changes will you make in your media choices after this evaluation? Why?**

Say: Evaluating our current media choices is one way we can make changes that will help us. ➤**God wants us to avoid harmful media choices. Another way to do this is to focus on God's Word and spiritual truths. Let's do that now.**

◄*The Point*

Life Application

The Word in Our Hearts *(up to 10 minutes)*

Have kids form four groups, and assign one of the four media choices from the previous activity to each group. Provide newsprint, markers, paper, and pens, along with Bibles, to groups. Ask a volunteer to read Deuteronomy 11:18-20 aloud. **Say: We aren't required to put God's Word on our hands or foreheads, but God does want us to have it in our hearts and minds. In your groups, create an expression of this verse from your assigned media choice. For example, you could write lyrics or create a rap using Deuteronomy 11:18-20 if you're the music media group. You can create a skit, write an advertising slogan, draw a picture of your idea, or come up with another creative idea!**

Allow groups about five minutes to create their presentations. Then have groups share their creative efforts.

Say: Great creative ideas! These ideas show how we are using God's Word to help us focus on positive media choices. Let's see how we can continue to do this.

Wrap-Up Option 1

Up With Media! *(up to 10 minutes)*

Say: Media does have some positive and helpful functions. For example, God has used the media to spread his message. It's also used to get useful information to people. Get in a circle, and brainstorm other positive aspects of the media.

Allow a few minutes for kids to work. Write preteens' responses on newsprint. Then close with prayer, asking God to help us focus on the positive things listed on the newsprint and to use discernment in making media choices.

Wrap-Up Option 2

Top Ten List *(up to 5 minutes)*

Say: Time for the Media Top Ten List! Let's brainstorm ten positive qualities of media. Call out the quality, and we'll allow some discussion before listing it.

Have preteens call out qualities. Allow some discussion if the quality doesn't quite make it, but keep the activity moving quickly. Allow about three minutes to create the list. Then have a closing prayer, having students say the listed qualities as part of the prayer.

Extra-Time Tips

Use these extra ideas to add some creative fun to your studies. They are low-prep or no-prep ideas that work in no time!

Music Talk—Have kids form pairs and carry on a one-minute conversation with each other using only titles and lyrics from their favorite songs. Allow volunteers to repeat their conversations for the rest of the class. Then have the pairs communicate using only verses and phrases from the Bible. Talk about the differences in the nature of the conversations.

Uplifting Flicks—Have preteens share a positive message they've received in movies they've seen. Have them share how it impacted their life or how the movie's message relates to this study's point.

Media Messages

Use Philippians 4:8-9 and these charts to evaluate the four media options listed below. Write down your media source in the blank, then place + or - signs in each of the boxes next to the spiritual trait from Philippians 4:8-9 according to that trait being included or excluded from your chosen media source.

Media:	TV	Movies and Videos/DVDs	Music	The Web and Computer Games
Source: _____	_____	_____	_____	

TV	Movies and Videos/DVDs	Music	The Web and Computer Games
True	True	True	True
Noble	Noble	Noble	Noble
Right	Right	Right	Right
Pure	Pure	Pure	Pure
Lovely	Lovely	Lovely	Lovely
Admirable	Admirable	Admirable	Admirable
Excellent	Excellent	Excellent	Excellent
Praiseworthy	Praiseworthy	Praiseworthy	Praiseworthy

When Life Goes Bad

The Point: ➤ God wants us to keep a good attitude during tough times.

A s they forge ahead on the journey toward adulthood, preteens may end up in the middle of difficult choices. And sometimes they make the wrong choices—and must suffer the consequences. Yet the consequences are harder to handle when the troubles are something beyond the preteens' control.

Use this study to help preteens develop healthy attitudes as they face difficult situations.

Scripture Source

Acts 16:16-34

Paul and Silas were spreading the good news of Jesus Christ in the Roman city of Philippi. In the course of their work, they cast a fortunetelling demon out of a slave girl. Her owners, angry that their source of income had been abruptly cut off, had Paul and Silas arrested, beaten, and thrown in jail. Yet, in spite of all this trouble, Paul and Silas spent the night singing and rejoicing in the Lord.

1 Peter 1:6-7

Peter wrote to Christians who were facing troublesome times. He reminded the early church that their joy didn't depend on outward circumstances but on inward joy. The trials they were encountering were refining them like pure gold. In addition, their relationship with Jesus could transform hardships into opportunities for rejoicing.

Section	Minutes	What Students Will Do	Supplies
Warm-Up Option 1	up to 10	**Exercise Fun!**—Compare exercising to fun.	
Warm-Up Option 2	up to 10	**Trash to Treasure**—Create something useful out of a bag of trash.	Prepared bags of trash (see p. 35)
Bible Connection	up to 15	**Instant Movie**—Write a film storyboard based on Paul's adventures in Acts 16.	Bibles, "Paul and Silas' Amazing Adventure Storyboard" handouts (p. 40), pens or fine-tipped markers
	up to 20	**Joyful Obstacles**—Maneuver through an obstacle course of tough situations and explore joyful responses to those situations.	Bibles, "Joyful Situations?" handout (p. 41), paper, pens, watch, scissors
Life Application	up to 10	**Joyful Shout!**—Brainstorm and shout out positive aspects of tough situations.	Newsprint, marker
Wrap-Up Option 1	up to 5	**When Life Gives You Lemons...**—Make and share lemonade.	Lemonade mix, water, pitcher, paper cups, lemon
Wrap-Up Option 2	up to 5	**Sweet Exchange**—Exchange "tough times" for lemon drops.	Slips of paper, pens, basket, lemon drops

Before the Study

Set out Bibles, prepared bags of trash (see "Trash to Treasure" activity), scissors, tape, paper, pens, watch with a second hand, newsprint, marker, a lemon, lemonade mix (or prepared beforehand), pitcher, cups, lemon drops, and a basket. Make one photocopy of the "Joyful Situations?" handout (p. 41). Also make enough photocopies of the "Paul and Silas' Amazing Adventure Storyboard" handout (p. 40) for each preteen to have one.

FYI

If you have jump ropes, dumbbells or other exercise equipment, it might be fun to use these. Also, you might want to have an exercise music CD or video (check for appropriateness first) playing during the exercise time.

The Study

Warm-Up Option 1

Exercise Fun! *(up to 10 minutes)*

Say: Let's begin by doing something that should be great fun—exercising!

With an enthusiastic manner, have the group stand up and participate in group exercises. Begin by jogging in place before leading them into a series of jumping jacks. Follow up with deep knee bends and push-ups.

After a few minutes of exercise, gather everyone in a circle.

Ask: • **How did you feel while you were exercising?**

• **Did you enjoy or not enjoy the exercises? Why?**

• **Why is exercise fun for some and not for others?**

Say: A person's attitude toward physical fitness will determine whether or not he or she enjoys exercising. Those who are serious about being healthy like to exercise, even though it can be exhausting. They know the end result will be good.

Sometimes in life we have to go through "exercises." These are the tough times we face. God cares when we face tough times. Even though it may not be easy, ➤God wants us to keep a good attitude when we face hard times. Today we're going to explore how to maintain that positive attitude during hard times.

◄ *The Point*

Warm-Up Option 2

Trash to Treasure *(up to 10 minutes)*

Collect several bags of "trash" before class. Include items such as old boxes, bottles, cans, pieces of newspaper, and string, but not leftover food items.

Form groups of up to five, and give each group a bag of prepared trash.

Ask: • **How many of you have heard of the phrase "One person's trash is another person's treasure"?**

Say: Today we are going to see if we can find some treasures in these bags of trash. As a group, dig through your trash bag, and use at least three items to create something useful. You'll have three minutes, so you'll need to work quickly. Ready? Go!

Allow preteens three minutes to work. Give kids a one-minute warning so they can wrap up their creation within the three minutes. After three minutes, give each group a chance to share its creation. Compliment groups on their creations.

Ask: • **What was it like to make something useful out of your trash?**

• **Did you think you could make anything useful out of your bag of trash? Why or why not?**

• **What kind of attitude did you have toward this task? Explain.**

Say: If I hadn't asked you to make something useful out of your trash, you would've just thought I was giving you bags of trash. Sometimes life gives us "bags of trash"—stuff that happens to us that we don't wish for. If you had a

good attitude turning your trash into something useful, you probably succeeded. In the same way, when we face hard times with a good attitude, we'll probably

The Point ➤ handle them better. Today we're going to look at how ➤God wants us to have a good attitude when we face hard times. Let's see why this is important.

Bible Connection

Instant Movie *(up to 15 minutes)*

Have preteens remain in their groups from the previous activity. Provide a Bible and a "Paul and Silas' Amazing Adventure Storyboard" handout (p. 40) for each student. Supply pens or fine-tipped markers.

Say: The Apostle Paul had his share of tough times. As he spread the good news about Jesus, he faced enough situations to make a great plot for an adventure movie. Congratulations! You are now movie producers! Before a movie is filmed, the people creating it draw up what is called a "storyboard." A storyboard is a series of rough sketches to show what they want in each scene. Today we are going to draw up a storyboard for this story out of Paul's life. Here's how to do it: Each of you has four storyboards to create. Decide in your group the order of your storyboards. Then read Paul's story in Acts 16:16-34, and create the scenes from the story on your handouts.

Allow preteens about five minutes to create their storyboards. Rotate among groups, and encourage them not to be too fancy with their art, just to get down on the paper what they would want a scene to show.

When everyone has finished or five minutes are up, allow volunteers from each group to share their storyboards with the larger group.

Ask: • How would you have felt if you had been in Paul's place in this situation?

• Which of the situations from Paul's life would have been hardest to have a positive attitude about? Explain.

• Why do you think Paul was able to find joy in the middle of his sufferings?

• How can our attitudes be like Paul's when we face hard times?

Say: Paul was able to find joy in tough situations. He understood how
The Point ➤ **➤God wants us to have positive attitudes when we face hard times.**

Now let's explore some tough situations and see how we would handle them.

Joyful Obstacles *(up to 20 minutes)*

Before your study, photocopy the "Joyful Situations?" handout (p. 41), and cut out the six situations. Place each situation, along with some blank paper and pens, at one of six stations you've set up around your room. Place a Bible open to 1 Peter 1:6-7 at each station.

Have a volunteer read aloud 1 Peter 1:6-7. Then have kids form groups of up to four. **Say: Now we're going to put into practice what the Bible verses talked about. I've set up around the room six stations that are part of a tough situations obstacle course. Each group will start at one station. You'll have two minutes at each station to read the situation and discuss how you could be joyful or find something good in that situation. Each group must come up with its own ideas, not ones from another group. You may reread 1 Peter 1:6-7 at any of the stations for guidance.**

Have each group choose a station, and begin timing the activity. Give groups two minutes at each station. Provide thirty-second countdown warnings. After all groups have rotated through the six stations, have them gather in their groups. Have groups discuss the questions listed below:

Ask: • How did you feel when dealing with the problems at each station?

• Which situation was the most difficult for your group? What made it hard?

• Were any of the situations easy to have a positive attitude about? Explain.

• What effect does attitude have when facing a hard situation?

Say: We may have gone through some of these situations or know people who have. ▶God wants us to have a good attitude when we face hard times. Let's practice this now.

Life Application

Joyful Shout! *(up to 10 minutes)*

Have kids form two teams, and label them Team 1 and Team 2. **Say: Having a positive attitude when we face tough times gives us the strength to handle the situation. Just as Paul and Silas were singing while in jail, we can have their same attitude. Team 1 will shout out a tough situation, such as divorced parents or a tough class at school. Then Team 2 will shout out one way they can have joy or find good in the situation and run up and write their response**

FYI

You may need to adjust this activity if you have fewer preteens. You could form pairs or have two or three groups go through only two or three situations, respectively.

FYI

Whenever groups discuss a list of questions, write the questions on newsprint, and tape the newsprint to the wall so that groups can discuss the questions at their own pace.

◀ *The Point*

on the newsprint. Then Team 2 will shout out another hard situation, and Team 1 will shout out a positive response and write their response on newsprint. We'll keep switching teams until each team has three responses listed on the newsprint. Ready? Go!

Allow teams to play until three responses are listed from each team.

Ask: • **Was it easy or hard to have a positive attitude during this game? Explain.**

• **How could friends help you deal with a hard situation?**

Say: God never intended for us to face tough times alone. Just as you worked together in your team to come up with positive responses, we can allow our friends to help us keep a positive attitude when those hard times come into our lives.

Wrap-Up Option 1

When Life Gives You Lemons... *(up to 5 minutes)*

Hold up a lemon.

Say: There is another old saying: When life gives you lemons...make lemonade! Let's do that now.

Have the ingredients gathered for lemonade, and prepare a pitcher (or have a pitcher prepared beforehand and bring it out). Distribute cups of lemonade. **Say:** Sometimes life is going to hand us lemons. There is no way around it. But we don't have to become sour people. With God's help, we can learn how to make lemonade out of the lemons we face.

Close with a prayer, asking God for strength and joy when tough times come.

Wrap-Up Option 2

Sweet Exchange *(up to 5 minutes)*

Hand a slip of paper and a pen to each student. Have each preteen write on a slip of paper one thing that he or she has difficulty maintaining a joyful attitude about.

Say: We will face things in our lives that leave us with a sour taste in our mouths. However, God is able to replace that sour taste with a sweet taste that can bring us joy. As a reminder of this truth, I will trade you a lemon drop for each slip of paper you have. The lemon drop may start out sour, but we all know that it's sweet inside.

As you collect the slips of paper in a basket, give each student a lemon drop or two. Then close with a prayer, asking God for help in finding joy in life's hard times.

Extra-Time Tips

Use these extra ideas to add some creative fun to your studies. They are low-prep or no-prep ideas that work in no time!

Tough Joy—Pair up your students. Instruct pairs each to make up an acronym based on the words *tough joy*. The acronym should reflect something they've learned from the study. An example might be:

T ry	J esus
O ut	O vercomes
U nderstanding	Y ucky stuff
G ood things, not	
H urts	

Tough Tests—Ask students to give examples of the toughest tests they have had to take in school. Then ask them to brainstorm good things that can or did come out of the tests. Next, discuss the kinds of "life tests" they will have to take long after school is over for them.

Paul and Silas' Amazing Adventure Storyboard

Joyful Situations?

You've been telling your non-Christian friend the importance of being honest, and you've just been caught cheating on a test.

Your best friend is moving out of the state.

Your parents have been fighting a lot lately, and they've just told you that they're getting divorced.

You were playing well on your team before the season started, but you've come down with a serious illness that will force you to miss most of the games.

You were arrested for shoplifting.

A bully at school has been picking **you** to beat up.

Changed 4 LiFE

This study has looked at helping preteens make great choices in the many situations they face. Use this retreat activity to reinforce the things learned in this study.

Choices, Choices Retreat

Design a retreat at which everything has choices that kids must make. You could start out with the big picture—allowing preteens to choose the retreat site or event. Following the site choice, you could include food choices at every meal, game choices, Bible study topic choices, even choices about shower times! Throughout the retreat, bring out the element of choice, and spend some time debriefing the variety of experiences during the retreat. At the conclusion of the retreat, you could offer a presentation of the greatest choice of all—the choice to believe in Jesus or commitment to follow him wholeheartedly.

EVALUATION FOR

Faith 4 Life: How to Make Great Choices

Please help Group Publishing, Inc., continue to provide innovative and useful resources for ministry. Please take a moment to fill out this evaluation and mail or fax it to us. Thanks!

Group Publishing, Inc.
Attention: Product Development
P.O. Box 481
Loveland, CO 80539
Fax: (970) 292-4370

● ● ●

1. As a whole, this book has been (circle one)
   not very helpful   *very helpful*
   1   2   3   4   5   6   7   8   9   10

2. The best things about this book:

3. Ways this book could be improved:

4. Things I will change because of this book:

5. Other books I'd like to see Group publish in the future:

6. Would you be interested in field-testing future Group products and giving us your feedback? If so, please fill in the information below:

Name _____

Church Name _____

Denomination _____ Church Size_____

Church Address _____

City_____ State _____ ZIP _____

Church Phone _____

E-mail _____

Look for the Whole Family of Faith 4 Life Bible Studies!

Preteen Books
Being Responsible
Getting Along With Others
God in My Life
Going Through Tough Times

How to Make Great Choices
Peer Pressure
The Bible and Me
Why God Made Me

Junior High Books
Becoming a Christian
Fighting Temptation
Finding Your Identity
Friends

God's Purpose for Me
My Life as a Christian
Understanding the Bible
Who Is God?

Senior High Books
Applying God's Word
Believing in Jesus
Family Matters
Is There Life After High School?

Prayer
Sexuality
Sharing Your Faith
Your Christian ID

Coming Soon...

For Preteens
Building Friendships
Handling Conflict

Succeeding in School
What's a Christian?

For Junior High
Choosing Wisely
How to Pray

My Family Life
Sharing Jesus

For Senior High
Christian Character
Following Jesus

Worshipping 24/7
Your Relationships

Visit your local Christian bookstore or contact Group Publishing, Inc. at 800-447-1070. www.grouppublishing.com

More Preteen Ministry Resources!

The Preteen Worker's Encyclopedia of Bible-Teaching Ideas

Make the New Testament come alive to your preteens and help them discover Bible truths in a big way! In this comprehensive collection, you get nearly 200 creative ideas and activities including: object lessons, skits, games, devotions, service projects, creative prayers, affirmations, creative readings, retreats, parties, trips and travel, and music ideas.

Flexible for any group setting, you'll easily find the perfect idea with helpful Scripture and theme indexes.

ISBN 0-7644-2425-4

Dynamic Preteen Ministry

Gordon West & Becki West

Maximize ministry to preteens as they make the difficult transition from childhood to adolescence. Both children's and youth workers will better understand the minds and emotions of 10- to 14-year-olds, "bridge the gap" between children's ministry and youth ministry.

ISBN 0-7644-2084-4

The Ultimate Book of Preteen Devotions

Take the challenge of ministering to preteens to the edge! They're sure to connect with these 75 Bible-based devotions. From setting goals, to materialism, to dealing with divorce—these topics and many others are included in the 6 big themes found in this ultimate book:

- Faith
- Friends
- Family
- School
- My World
- Special Days

Plus, easy-prep devotional activities use different learning styles—and multiple intelligences—to reach all preteens. Scripture index included.

ISBN 0-7644-2588-9

Order today from your local Christian bookstore, online at www.grouppublishing.com or write:
Group Publishing, P.O. Box 485, Loveland, CO 80539-0485.

Connect with Preteens In Dynamic Ways!

No-Miss Lessons for Preteen Kids

Here are 22 faith-building lessons that keep 5th- and 6th-graders coming back! Children's workers get active-learning lessons dealing with faith…self-esteem…relationships…choices…and age-appropriate service projects that any preteen class can do!

ISBN 0-7644-2015-1

No-Miss Lessons for Preteen Kids 2

Enjoy ministering to your preteens like never before! This flexible resource features 20 action-packed, easy-to-teach lessons that talk about the stuff of life in the preteen world. Stuff like the Internet and media, how to get along with family and friends, faith foundations based on God and Jesus, and many others! These lessons and the 13 bonus, "can't-miss" service project ideas will challenge kids, grow their faith, and give them practical ideas for living out their deepening faith in meaningful ways!

ISBN 0-7644-2290-1

The Ultimate Book of Preteen Games

They're not children. Not teenagers. What do you do with preteens? Have a blast! Start with these 100 games they'll love! In the process, you'll break down cliques, build relationships, explore relevant Bible truths, give thought-provoking challenges, and have high-energy fun!

ISBN 0-7644-2291-X

Order today from your local Christian bookstore, online at www.grouppublishing.com or write:
Group Publishing, P.O. Box 485, Loveland, CO 80539-0485.